ALL-PRO BASKETBALL STARS 1981

Bruce Weber

SCHOLASTIC BOOK SERVICES

New York Toronto London Auckland Sydney Tokyo

To Leonard Greene, who
started this journey long
ago in Ebbets Field

Material for All-Pro Basketball Stars 1981 went to
press on September 1, 1980. For each team's opening game roster, see page 91.

The author wishes to thank the public relations di-
rectors of the NBA teams and the league's media
department, who facilitated production of this
book.

Cover photo: Focus on Sports

ISBN 0-590-31936-1

12 11 10 9 8 7 6 5 4 3 2 1   1   1 2 3 4 5 6/8

Printed in the U. S. A.   06

CONTENTS

All-Pro Dan Roundfield is the
key to the Hawks' 1981
championship hopes.

1980 ALL-PRO TEAM

Forward: Julius Erving
Forward: Dan Roundfield
Forward: Marques Johnson
Forward: Walter Davis
  Center: Kareem Abdul-Jabbar
  Center: Moses Malone
  Guard: George Gervin
  Guard: Gus Williams
  Guard: Paul Westphal
  Guard: Dennis Johnson

JULIUS ERVING
Philadelphia 76ers

NBA players take nearly 150,000 shots every season. It's practically impossible to select the best one. But everyone is still talking about the basket Dr. J scored against the Lakers in last season's playoffs.

The Doctor, still the most exciting player in the game, swooped in on the right side of the Laker hoop. Six feet out, he took off, only to find way blocked by 7-2 Kareem Abdul-Jabbar. The 6-6 Doctor never hesitated, still floating in the air, he swooped around, behind the backboard and around the bucket, then flipped the ball back and into the basket. The videotape of the amazing shot made the 11 o'clock news everywhere for days afterward.

Julius Erving's fans take those kinds of amazing moves for granted. They've seen the 30-year-old, 10-year-veteran handle a basketball—and his body—with uncanny skill since his earliest days as a pro.

After a so-so (for him) 1979 season, Doc bounced back with another incredible year in 1980. His 26.9 ppg scoring average was his best ever since joining the NBA for the 1977 campaign. It was easily the Sixers' best (Darryl Dawkins was second with 14.7). His 170 steals placed him among NBA ball-thieves. He also blocked 140 shots, only two less than Dawkins who is nearly six inches taller!

The playoff loss to Los Angeles spoiled what might have been Dr. J's finest pro season. But no one in Philly is knocking the Doctor. He averaged 24.4 ppg in the post-season action, leading the Sixers past Washington, Atlanta, and arch-rival Boston before the six-game loss to the Lakers. The Doc, a two-time ABA champion with the New York Nets, would really like an NBA trophy to complete his home decorations.

Forward
DAN ROUNDFIELD
Atlanta Hawks

The No-Names finally have a name. Not a household name, except in the Atlanta area. But a name. An All-Pro name.

The name is Roundfield, as in Dan Roundfield. And if he isn't a household name around your household, you're probably not the basketball fan you thought you were.

For years, Atlanta coach Hubie Brown turned out playoff teams with men only their mothers could love. But Roundfield, who came to Georgia as an Indiana free agent, has changed all that.

Powerful at 6-8 and 205 pounds, Dan doesn't project the tough guy image you might expect from a power forward. He looks soft and talks soft. But on the court, he's all nails.

Funny thing about it, some fans, even in Atlanta, don't recognize Roundfield's skill. They stuffed the All-Star ballot boxes for his teammate John Drew. And guard Eddie Johnson won the team MVP award. But night in and night out, it's the 27-year-old Roundfield who gets things done.

His 16.5 ppg scoring in 1980 set an all-time personal record. And though he dropped out of the NBA's top ten in rebounding and blocked shots, he did manage a 10.3 per game rebound mark (11th in the league) and 139 blocks (12th in the league).

Roundfield didn't play organized basketball until his junior year of high school — and then for a team which lost every game. He showed enough improvement as a senior to be contacted by a half-dozen colleges, including Central Michigan. There, Dan became the star of a team which won the Mid-American Conference title and went to the NCAA tournament.

Dan's only weakness? His injuries. Last season it was a torn lower back muscle — which didn't keep him out of the line-up. Earlier a broken wrist — broken four times — caused him to miss 42 games in two years. That's why Dan wears such heavy tape on his wrists.

Forward
MARQUES JOHNSON
Milwaukee Bucks

Dennis and Magic and Eddie and the rest forgive us, we'll take Milwaukee's Marques as the captain of our all-Johnson

6

team. As a matter of fact, Marques can be the captain of just about any team he wants.

It's just possible that the 3-year-veteran from UCLA is the best all-around player in the league. Nobody does so many things as well as the muscular Marques. The 6-7, 218-pounder possesses great strength, quickness, and spring. He shoots, passes, rebounds, and plays defense with the best. And what he doesn't do very well, he does pretty well.

Despite a bout with the flu and a strained back last season, Marques still led the Bucks in scoring (21.7 ppg, the league's 14th best total). That total might have been higher, but the addition of burly Bob Lanier at mid-season took some of the scoring pressure off Johnson. Marques responded by dishing out 4.2 assists per game after the All-star break, compared with 3.3 before it.

Johnson is one of the all-time best shooters. His lifetime 53.9% mark is the fourth best ever (behind leader Wilt Chamberlain).

As you'd expect, Marques has lots of fans in Milwaukee. You might not expect that he also has a lot of fans around the rest of the league. Hear Chicago coach, Jerry Sloan: "I can't believe how hard Marques works. What an exciting player he is. I love to see him play—if we aren't playing against him."

Marques, who moved directly from college star to pro star, was surprised that he made the adjustment so quickly. He's one of the few who is.

WALTER DAVIS
Phoenix Suns

If this is the Phoenix Suns' year — and with their personnel it might just be—then Walter Davis is going to enjoy his fourth pro season. In three NBA seasons, Davis has been a top scorer, an All-Star every year, and a team player beyond compare. But he still hasn't picked up an NBA title— and he misses it.

With Paul Westphal gone to Seattle, more offensive pressure than ever falls on the broad shoulders of the 6-6, 198-pounder from North Carolina. Sweet D's scoring dipped a bit last season, to a not too shabby 21.5 ppg. That ranked him 15th in the NBA and second (to Westphal) among the Suns. But the addition of defensive-minded Dennis (D. J.) Johnson (in the Westphal trade) means that Phoenix will probably require at least 24 ppg from the 26-year-old Davis.

Walt thinks he can handle it, and the stat sheets prove that he can. The 1978 Rookie of the Year hit for 24.2 ppg during his freshman pro season (with 23.6 his second year).

Any coach, including the Suns' John McLeod, can use Davis' game films as a perfect illustration of the ideal small forward. Walt is beautiful to watch — unless you happen to be the guy assigned to guard him. Like a fluid ballet dancer, Sweet D moves with amazing grace. His jump shot, deadly from anywhere inside the top of the key, is straight out of a basketball textbook. He's just as dangerous when he goes to the hoop, especially at the end of a fast break.

The 1976 Olympic gold-medal winner hit 56.3% of his field goal attempts in '80, an all-time personal high. He also finished second on the club in assists (4.5 per game) and steals (1.52). And is he consistent? He hit in double figures in 74 of his 75 outings.

The pro's pro. That's Walt Davis.

Center
KAREEM ABDUL-JABBAR
Los Angeles Lakers

Just when you think—and the opponents hope—that Kareem Abdul-Jabbar is ready to slip back into the world of "human" players, the Lakers' main man goes out and enjoys another superhuman year.

That's the way it was a year ago. Kareem, now 33 years old, had lost his crown as the NBA's top center to Houston's

Moses Malone. And the Lakers had failed to win a championship for the seventh straight year.

Enter Magic Johnson and a pumped up more mature, more open, more enthusiastic Kareem and, presto, a sixth MVP Award for the 7-2 (or more) former UCLA star and an NBA title for the new Lakers.

Kareem's eleventh season as a pro (he started with the Milwaukee Bucks) was one of his best. The king of the sky-hook played 38.3 minutes per game (not bad for an aging star), tossed in 24.8 points per game (sixth in the league), pulled down 10.8 rebounds per contest, and continued to do all those things that make him perhaps the greatest ever.

Best of all, Kareem seemed to enjoy playing last year more than ever. He played very hard, diving after loose balls, racing up the court to lead or even break up a fast break. "By the numbers," says Laker coach Paul Westhead, "it wasn't Kareem's best year. He didn't average close to his lifetime 28.3 ppg. He didn't grab 1,000 rebounds for only the third time in his career. But I can't believe he has ever played harder than he did last season."

Westhead is probably right. The new Kareem is a cross between "Mr. Clutch" and "Charlie Hustle." He now seems to hit more shots, block more shots, and hit the open man when the chips are down than anytime during his fabulous career. The prospect for more years of the same is frightening — at least to the rest of the clubs in the NBA West.

MOSES MALONE

Houston Rockets

In Dublin, as the old song says, sweet
Molly Malone did her thing with cockles
and mussels. In Houston, sweet Moses
Malone does his with slam-dunks and rebounds. In her best year, it's doubtful that

Molly ever came close to Moses' million-dollar-a-year payoff. But how many points-per-game did she average?

Moses, the young (25-years-old) sixth-year-man, quietly does it all for the Rockets. The powerful 6-10, 235-pounder is the best offensive rebounder in the universe. Though he lost the NBA rebound title to San Diego's Swen Nater (15.0 to 14.5 per game), Moses grabbed off 573 offensive rebounds. He turns every Rocket mis-fire into an adventure.

Malone, who turned pro straight out of Petersburg (Va.) High School, had his best scoring year in '80. His 25.8 ppg scoring, his best ever, was good for sixth in the NBA. Opponents find him impossible to stop. Coming into the 1980-81 season, Moses had scored in double-figures (10 or more points) in 155 straight regular-season games. And he grabbed 10 or more rebounds in 71 of the Rockets' 82 games last year.

Everyone in Houston loves Big Mo. He plays hard every night. "Sure it's frustrating when you have a big night but you lose," he says. "But I know my teammates are trying hard too. So you forget about it and try even harder the next game."

Rocket traveling secretary Dick Vandervoort is one of Mo's biggest fans. "He has never caused a single problem," he says. "Some superstars think they deserve special treatment. But not Malone. I don't think anyone's told him yet that he is a superstar."

If not, Moses Malone may be the last to find out!

GEORGE GERVIN
San Antonio Spurs

In Texas, where they do things bigger (and, they say, better) than anywhere else, George Gervin fits in perfectly. He scores points more often than any guard in basketball history. And thanks to his rich contract, he'll continue to do his thing in San Antonio for years to come.

The man knows how to put the ball in

the bucket. His 33.1 ppg scoring was the best of his career and was good enough to win his third straight NBA scoring title. Let's try to put that in perspective. No guard had ever won as many as two straight point crowns. And only four players have ever won as many as three.

As you might imagine, defense isn't George's strong suit. But the 6-7, 185-pound "Iceman" more than makes up for it on the San Antonio end of the floor. Last season, in addition to his 33.1 points, he hit on 52.8% of his field goal attempts while picking up 202 assists, averaging 5.2 rebounds, even blocking 79 shots, high among the Spurs.

"I know he averages about 25 shots a game," says Boston's Chris Ford. "But they're just about all good. I've never seen him force a shot. He's no gunner."

On offense, Ice can do it all. No one can stop him one-on-one. He has the uncanny ability to decide what to do with the ball in mid-air. He drives better than any car you've ever seen and he can use both hands extremely well.

No matter what the situation, the Spurs count on George. He has scored in double-figures in 141 straight games and had 20 or more in 74 of his 78 games in 1980. He virtually owns the Spurs' record book setting three new marks and bettering 18 of his own last year.

New Spurs' coach Stan Albeck has a tough job ahead of him. But with Gervin's 30 or so points in the bank before every game starts, the job becomes just a little easier.

GUS WILLIAMS
Seattle SuperSonics

Gus Williams spent his summer talking money with his bosses at Seattle. Considering that Gus already was being paid about a quarter of a million dollars a year, you might wonder what he was yelling about. But since NBA players *average* about $150,000 each, Gus had a great point.

The 27-year-old, who has led Seattle in scoring for three straight seasons, is just about the quickest player anywhere moving with the ball. "That's the key for me," says the 6-2, 175-pounder from Mount Vernon, N.Y. "I'm not the greatest shooter. I'm not the greatest passer. And I'm not the greatest rebounder. But I am quick and I think I can lead a fast break as well as anyone. Sure I make mistakes sometimes, but I usually make up for them."

Originally drafted by Golden State, Gus was considered a problem child by the Warriors. Seattle picked him up as a free agent in '77, and haven't looked back.

Older brother of the Knicks' Ray Williams, Gus has been the Sonics' top scorer in each of his three seasons, racking up his best season (22.1 ppg) last year. That was good enough for 11th place in the league, just one spot ahead of his newest teammate, Paul Westphal. Gus also had 2.44 steals per game, the NBA's fourth highest total.

Unlike many pro stars, Gus prefers to stay out of the public eye. "It's tough," he says, "especially in a place like Seattle. But I think it's tough enough producing on the court without the extra pressure of public appearances."

It may take some time for Williams to blend in with Westphal (who replaces Dennis Johnson in the Seattle backcourt). But Gus says he's ready, and that's good enough for the Sonics and their fans.

PAUL WESTPHAL
Seattle SuperSonics

In basketball, as in everything else, you can't get something for nothing. So when Seattle decided it needed Phoenix all-pro Paul Westphal to help it return to the top of the NBA heap, the price was expensive. The Sonics had to part with their own all-pro, Dennis (D. J.) Johnson.

The truth is, neither Westphal nor Johnson were overly happy in their old homes. Perhaps the change of scenery will do them both a lot of good.

It won't be easy for Westphal, the 6-4, 195-pounder from Southern Cal, to get much better. His 21.9 ppg average, best on the Suns for the fifth straight year, was the 12th best in the NBA. He also led the Suns in assists for the fourth year in a row and set a Phoenix single-game record by tossing in 49 points against Detroit last February. That's firepower.

And firepower is exactly what Seattle coach Len Wilkens hopes the 30-year-old Westphal delivers to the Kingdome. "We needed an outside threat to help our offense," says Wilkens. "We feel that Paul's all-around play will blend perfectly with what we have."

Sonics' fans may end up calling Westphal, "Old Reliable." Paul has hit more than half of his shots as a pro, even more when the game is on the line. He goes to the hoop extremely well and works well with both hands. On defense, he's one of the smartest players in the league.

Is Westphal happy to be in Seattle. You bet. "My five years in Phoenix were great," he says. "But Seattle has a real shot at the title. I'm looking forward to it."

19

Guard
DENNIS JOHNSON
Phoenix Suns

D. J.'s life changed last summer during a visit to the Philippines. Nothing happened there, however. But during Dennis Johnson's trans-Pacific visit he learned he had been traded from the Seattle Super-Sonics to the Suns.

Johnson's departure from Seattle was a forgone conclusion. Because of Dennis' moodiness, his game was suffering, said Seattle officials. The only question: where to send him and for whom?

The answers were Phoenix and Paul Westphal. "We gave up some offense," says Phoenix general manager, Jerry Colangelo. "But we picked up lots more, things that we really needed."

Colangelo means things like defense, shot-blocking, and rebounding. D.J., a super-quick 6-4, 185-pounder, is just about the best defensive guard in the world. For most players, it takes a spectacular scoring night to turn a game around. With D.J., his defense can do it.

The 26-year-old — four years younger than Westphal — has a great feel for defense. "I worked very hard on 'D' in both junior college and college," he says. "I figured I'd have a better chance as a defensive expert."

But though Johnson's 42.2% shooting was the NBA's worst (among starters) last year, he can also make things happen when his team has the ball. His 18.9 ppg average in '79 was his best ever, and he's great on the wing of a fast break.

The big question in Phoenix: will D.J. have his head on straight? Suns coach John McLeod, a great leader, isn't worried.

Trade a star and two top draft
picks for a rookie? The Blazers
did — for 6-6 Calvin Natt — and
they're delighted!

1980
ALL-ROOKIE
TEAM

Forward: **Larry Bird**
Forward: **Calvin Natt**
Center: **Bill Cartwright**
Guard: **Earvin (Magic) Johnson**
Guard: **Dudley Bradley**

Forward
LARRY BIRD
Boston Celtics

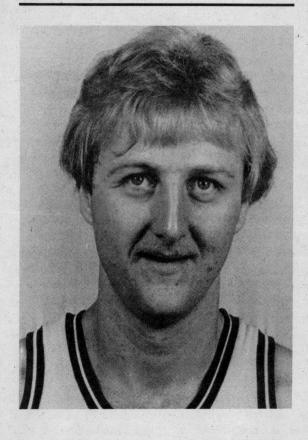

Larry Bird had every reason to disappoint Boston Celtics fans last season. When he signed with the Celts — for $650,000 a year — after being drafted the previous season, Boston rooters felt sure he'd be the guy who would turn around the last-place team. Never has so large a group set itself up for such a major failure.

But there was no failure. Larry, the 6-9 forward from Indiana State, was everything he was advertised to be—and more. "He's probably the best rookie since Bill Walton," said Utah boss Tom Nissalke. If anything, it was an understatement. Ex-Detroit coach Richie Adubato put it a little better. "If he gets any better," he said, after a 41-point Bird effort, "he'll have invented a new game."

From the season's opening tip-off, every Celtic opponent keyed on the new man. It didn't help. Larry led the Bostonians in just about every department, including minutes played, field goals attempted and made, free throws attempted and made, assists, and scoring. Rarely has a rookie done so much so often.

Some experts had doubts about Larry's shooting ability and speed before his debut. He squashed these doubts instantly. In fact, his quickness turned out to be one of his greatest assets. And he's tough. A couple of rivals tested him early, and he passed with flying colors. End of test.

If Larry has one complaint, it's finishing second. His Indiana State team lost to Michigan State in the finals of the 1979 NCAA championships. And the Celts lost to Philadelphia in the finals of the 1980 NBA Eastern playoffs. Maybe the Rookie of the Year voting—Larry won by a mile—is the start of something big for Boston's real Big Bird.

Forward
CALVIN NATT
Portland Trail Blazers

It takes a special rookie to command a
former all-pro and a pair of first-round
draft choices in the trade market. Calvin

Natt is special. About two-thirds of the way through the season, the New Jersey Nets decided they'd rather have tough Maurice Lucas and two first-rounders instead of Calvin. Expensive, yes. But Calvin's new employers, the Portland Trail Blazers, think he's worth it.

Natt, a muscular 6-6, 220-pounder from Northeast Louisiana, made just one mistake last season. He picked the same rookie year as Larry Bird, Magic Johnson, and Bill Cartwright. Otherwise, he might have had a real shot at the Rookie of the Year award.

Natt did well in New Jersey and even better in Portland. The Nets expected him to produce right away, and he did — on offense and defense. Trouble was, the team wasn't very good and not many fans around the league realized how large Natt's contribution was.

They understood right away in Portland. In 25 games with the Blazers, he tossed in 20.4 points per game, hit 48% from the field, and 77% from the foul line. Each figure was better than Calvin's New Jersey numbers.

Everyone figured Calvin would score. He averaged 23.9 ppg in college. But his defense was the most pleasant surprise. His Net coach, Kevin Loughery, said, "He's as good a defensive player as I've ever seen come into the league."

That's high praise from a defensive-oriented coach like Loughery. But Portland boss Jack Ramsay loves good "D" too. He can't wait to have Calvin for a full season with the Blazers.

BILL CARTWRIGHT

New York Knickerbockers

Bill Cartwright just isn't lucky. Anytime a rookie can lead his team in scoring with a 21.7 ppg average, in rebounding with 726, even in shooting with 54.7%, he should have an outstanding shot at Rookie of the Year honors. But not if he breaks in with Larry Bird and Magic Johnson.

To his credit, Cartwright played basketball's toughest position and played it every night. He averaged 38½ minutes, a rough haul for anyone, especially a 22-year-old rookie. The last rookie center to rack up Cartwright's kind of numbers? It was Kareem Abdul-Jabbar (then Lew Alcindor) 10 years earlier.

Most New York fans developed an immediate love affair with the former San Francisco star. In previous years, the Knicks didn't score much. They just tried to get a point or two more than the opponents. With Cartwright, they became the league's fourth highest-scoring team. They played exciting basketball. Only the NBA's tie-breaking rules kept them out of the post-season playoffs.

Cartwright's problem — like most of his teammates — came on defense. The Knicks ranked 20th in that department, with too little help from the big man in the middle. Bill's difficulty might have stemmed from the excess baggage (weight) he was toting around.

Still, he impressed observers all over the league. "He improved in every department during the season," said Philly coach Billy Cunningham. "He doesn't have a lot of great moves," says Houston's Billy Paultz, "but he really makes out with those he has."

Cartwright, whose major off-court interests are music and chess, was always a great shooter, even as a 6-9 high school sophomore in tiny Elk Grove, CA. At San Francisco U., he continued the offensive show, though he was never able to match the NCAA titles of a previous USF center, Bill Russell.

Guard
EARVIN (MAGIC) JOHNSON
Los Angeles Lakers

In Los Angeles, the city of stars, few shine brighter than the Lakers' magic man, "Magic" Johnson. You can call him Magic, or you can call him E. J., or you can call him J. J., or you can call him what the Lakers' NBA opponents call him, pure poison. Anyway you have it, the biggest guard (6-8, 215 pounds) in captivity has a way of making things happen on a basketball court.

You only have to think back to the sixth game of last year's final-round playoffs. L. A. led three to two, but with Kareem Abdul-Jabbar on the sidelines, everyone's bags were packed for the trip back to Hollywood and Game 7. Everyone but Magic. He had his hometown, East Lansing, Mich., on his mind. He wanted to go home. So Magic poured in 42 points, played a flawless floor game, and Kareem, at home and in bed, became an absentee NBA champion.

Maybe the Lakers ought to rename Magic, "Happy." Few players have ever enjoyed playing the game like the 21-year-old Johnson, who passed up his last two years at Michigan State for a shot at the pros. The smile on his face isn't forced, it's natural. It's always there. Even when he's victimized by a full-court press by radio, TV, and newspaper people, he's delighted.

"I enjoy talking basketball," he says, "and I enjoy talking about our team. We play the kind of basketball I like to play. And you can't beat that."

Magic's only problem for 1981: What can he do for an encore? In the last four years, he has won a state high school championship, a national college championship, and a world pro title. What's next?

"I want to win the whole thing every year," he says. And though no team has managed to win even two straight titles in more than a decade, no one is arguing with "Magic" Johnson.

DUDLEY BRADLEY

Indiana Pacers

New Pacer coach Jack McKinney has to
love Dudley Bradley. McKinney, who led
the Lakers for 13 games last season before
a biking accident ended his year, takes

over a club that isn't nearly as talented as the one he left in L. A. But a guard like Bradley helps to close some of that gap.

Dudley, a 6-6, 195-pounder, is the latest in the long line of products off the Dean Smith-U. of North Carolina assembly line. Seems that the Tar Heels always turn out a standout pro freshman — Walter Davis, Phil Ford, and Bradley being the last three.

Bradley, MVP of the 1979 Atlantic Coast Conference Tournament, played in every Pacer game last year, averaging nearly 25 minutes per outing. That makes his 8.4 ppg scoring average seem disappointing. But that's what everyone expected of Bradley. In college, he was known as "The Secretary of Defense," and the label continues to follow him in the pros.

Bradley, who started 37 games for Indiana in 1980, registered at least one steal in 72 of the Pacers' 82 games. His 211 steals, an average of 2.57 per game, placed him third in the NBA, behind the Knicks' Mike Richardson and the Nets' Eddie Jordan.

The San Antonio Spurs would be quite happy if Dudley had stayed in North Carolina. He did his best work against them. On March 28, he hit a career-high 22 points in a game with the Spurs after setting a one-game high of seven steals against them on October 27, 1979.

The 23-year-old played the same way at North Carolina. In his senior year he averaged only 9.3 ppg but registered 97 steals in only 29 games. That's more than three per game.

The brightest light in the
Valley of the Sun: it's 6-6
All-Pro Walter (Sweet D) Davis
of Phoenix.

A LOOK BACK—
A LOOK AHEAD

(Team statistical leaders must
meet NBA minimum qualification
standards.)

BOSTON CELTICS

Dave Cowens   **Chris Ford**

The team with the best record in the NBA a year ago gets mixed reviews. Boston's 61-21 mark was one win better than eventual champ Los Angeles and two better than East rival Philadelphia. But when the dust cleared last spring, it was L. A. vs. Philly for all the marbles. Regular season records in the NBA are meaningless.

Then general manager Red Auerbach tried to full-court press Virginia U. star Ralph Sampson into turning pro. (Boston owned the No. 1 draft choice.) After a lot of wheeling and dealing, Sampson stayed in Charlottesville and Auerbach swapped the top pick.

The Celts didn't make out too badly. Golden State gave them center Robert Parish, the 7-0 still-could-make-it center, and a draft pick who turned out to be Kevin McHale, a 6-11 rock from Minnesota.

Elsewhere, the Celts did well. Both 6-1

Tiny Archibald (14.1), the 1980 comeback kid, and 6-8 Cornbread Maxwell (16.9) tested the free-agent waters and decided to return to Boston. 6-9 Larry Bird (21.3), who enjoyed the kind of rookie season most players just dream about, should join Bob Cousy and Bill Russell in Boston's all-time Hall of Fame by the time he's 26 or so. The guy is unbelievable.

At age 32, 6-8½ Dave Cowens still does amazing things. He doesn't have to do it for 48 minutes anymore, and he's grateful that Bill Fitch, not he, is doing the coaching. But he's always a force the opponents must contend with. Vet 6-5 Chris Ford (11.2) is an outstanding shooter. The Boston-Philly Atlantic chase could be a corker.

TEAM LEADERS—1980

Minutes Played: Bird, 2,955
Field-Goal Percentage: Maxwell, .609
Three-Point Percentage: Ford, .427
Free-Throw Percentage: Bird, .836
Scoring: Bird, 21.3

Rebounds: Bird, 852
Assists: Archibald, 671
Steals: Bird, 143
Blocks: Cowens, 61

DRAFT CHOICES

1.	Kevin McHale	6-11	Minnesota
2.	Arnett Hallman	6-7	Purdue
3.	Ron Perry	6-1	Holy Cross
3a.	Don Newman	6-3	idaho
4.	Kevin Hamilton	6-3	Iona
5.	Rufus Harris	6-4	Maine
6.	Kenny Evans	6-3	Norfolk St.
7.	Les Henson	6-5	Virginia Tech
8.	Steve Wright	6-8	Boston U
9.	Brian Jung	7-0	Northwestern
10.	John Nolan	6-3	Providence

PHILADELPHIA 76ERS

Bobby Jones

Darryl Dawkins

The Sixers still can't believe they lost Game 6 of the NBA finals to the Jabbar-less Lakers last spring. They'll be out to make sure it doesn't happen again this time.

As long as coach Billy Cunningham has his hands on basketball's most exciting guided missile, Julius Erving, the Sixers will be in the title hunt. The 6-6 Doctor, who leaps out of buldings, does amazing things, including scoring 26.9 ppg, fourth best in the league.

"Chocolate Thunder," 6-11½ Darryl Dawkins, set the hoop world abuzz last winter by smashing two backboards (Kansas City and Philadelphia) within three weeks. The 14.7 ppg scorer, a five-year-vet at age 23, can actually scatter glass whenever he wants to. His partner in Philly's "Gruesome Twosome," 7-0 center-forward Caldwell Jones, led the team in

38

rebounding (fourth in the league) and rejections (seventh in the NBA). Dawkins-Jones is a scary combination.

6-9 defensive whiz Bobby Jones (13.0) is a perfect third to the "Gruesome Twosome," and 6-8 Steve Mix (11.6), one of the game's hardest workers, provides depth.

Bone spurs, a broken bone, and a torn knee ligament all ruined 6-7 Doug Collins (13.8) 1980 season after only 36 performances. Though 6-1 Mo Cheeks (11.4) and new Sixer 6-3 Lionel Hollins (12.2 in 27 games) held up the backcourt without Collins (and with help from 6-1 Henry Bibby, a 9.0 scorer), a healthy Collins would help. Color Philly dangerous!

TEAM LEADERS — 1980

Minutes Played: Erving, 2,812
Field-Goal Percentage: Cheeks, .540
Three-Point Percentage: DNQ*
Free-Throw Percentage: Mix, .831[a]

Rebounds: C. Jones, 950
Assists: Cheeks, 556
Steals: Cheeks, 183
Blocks: C. Jones, 162

Scoring: Erving, 26.9

*No 76er made the 25 3-pt. goals needed to qualify.
[a]Doug Collins (113 of 124 for .911) did not qualify.

DRAFT CHOICES

1.	Andrew Toney	6-3	Southwestern La.
1a.	Monti Davis	6-6½	Tennessee St.
2.	Clyde Austin	6-2	N. C. State
3.	Reggie Gaines	6-6	Winston-Salem (NC) State
4.	Billy Bryant	6-4	Western Kentucky
4a.	Harold Hubbard	6-6	Savannah St.
5.	Jim Swaney	6-7	Toledo
6.	Donald Cooper	6-7	St. Augustine's (NC)
7.	Richard Smith	7-1	Weber St.
8.	Martin Lemelle	6-2	Grambling
9.	Luke Griffin	6-1	St. Joseph's (Pa.)
10.	Joe Hand	6-0	King's (Pa.)

WASHINGTON BULLETS

Greg Ballard   Elvin Hayes

Who said that you can't go home again? (Actually, it was Thomas Wolfe.) Gene Shue, the new Bullets' coach, doesn't agree. The Baltimore native, U. of Maryland grad, and former Bullet coach is back for his second go-round, after stops in Philadelphia and San Diego.

Shue has a tough job ahead. The Bullets have made the playoffs twelve straight times (since 1969). But last year was the closest call of all. Washington's 39-43 mark tied them with the Knicks for the final playoff berth. It took the NBA's tie-breaking procedures to secure the spot for Washington.

Shue's team is aging, no doubt about it. Captain Wes Unseld is 34, with knees that are closer to 50. Still he played in all 82 games, had his best rebounding year since 1973 (1,094, third best in the league), and handed off assists like a rookie.

Elvin Hayes, the seemingly ageless 6-9 forward, also seems to improve with age. Though he turned 35 during the first month of this season, he comes off another banner year (eighth in the NBA in scoring — 23.0, fifth in rebounding — 896, and fifth in blocked shots — 2.33).

Can these men continue to perform at their rather advanced (for basketball) ages? Shue hopes so.

6-5 Kevin Grevey (14.0) is a sharp-shooting guard, who finished strong after missing some early action with a pulled hamstring. 6-7 Greg Ballard (15.6) got a chance to start when Bob Dandridge banged up his right leg early last season.

Look for Shue to clear some of the team's trouble-makers off the roster.

TEAM LEADERS — 1980

Minutes Played: Hayes, 3,183
Field-Goal Percentage: Unseld, .513
Three-Point Percentage: Grevey, .370
Free-Throw Percentage: Grevey, .867
Scoring: Hayes, 23.0

Rebounds: Unseld, 1,094
Assists: Porter, 457
Steals: Ballard, 90
Blocks: Hayes, 189

DRAFT CHOICES

1.	Wes Matthews	6-1	Wisconsin
2.	Ricky Mahorn	6-10	Hampton (Va.) Inst.
4.	Francois Wise	6-6	Long Beach St.
5.	Daryl Strickland	6-5	Rutgers
6.	Ken Dancy	6-5	Chicago St.
7.	Karl Godine	6-4	S. F. Austin
8.	Rich Valavicius	6-5	Auburn
9.	Clinton Wyatt	6-5	Alcorn St. (Miss.)
10.	Don Youman	6-7	Oklahoma St.

41

NEW YORK KNICKERBOCKERS

Ray Williams

Toby Knight

The future in New York looks better though not necessarily bright. Some of the Knicks' young people show promise, but not enough to require the team to start printing championship tickets.

Big 6-11 Bill Cartwright was the NBA's No. 3 rookie a year ago, though he wasn't in the class of Larry Bird and "Magic" Johnson. The San Francisco grad averaged 21.7 ppg (13th in the league), but he was only so-so on defense and was not among the top rebounders. Some fans wonder if Bill was too heavy.

Fast-hands Michael Ray Richardson added league assists (10.1 per game) and steals (3.23 per game) titles to his 15.3 ppg scoring. His problem: turnovers — including a team-high 359 in 82 games.

Richardson's backcourt partner, Ray Williams (20.9) was on the trading block all summer as the Knicks searched for a good small forward. Ex-Cavalier all-star 6-8 Campy Russell (18.2) replaces injured 6-9 Toby Knight at big forward. Rookie 6-9 Larry Demic, a surprise first-round choice in the '79 draft, played in all 82 games and averaged 7.0 ppg while learning to play facing the basket. 7-0 Marvin Webster, out for 62 of the Knicks' 82 a year ago, could be a tremendous help if healthy.

Despite the search for an experienced small forward, coach Red Holzman hopes that top draft-pick Mike Woodson of Indiana can fill the bill. No matter, Philly and Boston are out of the Knicks' sight.

TEAM LEADERS — 1980

Minutes Played: Cartwright, 3,150
Field-Goal Percentage: Cartwright, .547
Three-Point Percentage: Richardson, .245
Free-Throw Percentage: Knight, .808

Rebounds: Cartwright, 726
Assists: Richardson, 832
Steals: Richardson, 265
Blocks: Meriweather, 120

Scoring: Cartwright, 21.7

DRAFT CHOICES

1.	Mike Woodson	6-5	Indiana
2.	DeWayne Scales	6-9	LSU
3.	Kurt Rambis	6-8	Santa Clara
4.	Joe Crnelich	6-7	Wisconsin
5.	William Carey	6-4	Albright
6.	Kelvin Hicks	6-7	N.Y. Tech
7.	Bobby Turner	6-4	Louisville
8.	James Salters	5-10	Penn
9.	Don Wiley	6-7	Monmouth (NJ)
10.	Gerald Ross	6-8	Grand Canyon

NEW JERSEY NETS

Maurice Lucas   **Ed Jordan**

To Nets fans, their favorites are an all-out, hard-fighting, no-nonsense bunch of defensive aces. To the opponents, they're just the gang that couldn't shoot straight. True, the Nets' 34-48 record in 1980 was the best last-place mark in the league. But it was still a last-place mark, and the New Jerseyans would like to improve on that in their final year before their new home in the Jersey Meadowlands is ready.

Chances are they won't. The rest of the division is loaded and, in most cases, improving.

Top draftees Mike O'Koren of North Carolina and Mike Gminski of Duke, both products of the rugged Atlantic Coast Conference, are Kevin's type of players. But like the rest of their teammates, their shooting ability is suspect.

Hard-nosed Mike Newlin, who arrived in New Jersey from Houston last fall, had a bang-up season (20.9) offensively and defensively. Maurice Lucas (14.7, but 15.2 as a Net) arrived from Portland as a sure-thing, but the price (future star Calvin Natt) was expensive.

Fast Eddie Jordan (13.3) was second in the league in steals (2.72) and ninth in assists (6.8). He's the key to the backcourt, unless he's traded for some up-front strength. 6-8 Jan van Breda Kolff (6.8) is one of those great "D", no "O" Nets. But every time you write him off, he bounces back. Key to the Nets' front-court is former Southern Cal star Cliff Robinson who proved he could play as a rookie with a 13.6 ppg average and 506 rebounds .

Another tough year for the Nets?

TEAM LEADERS — 1980

Minutes Played: Jordan, 2,657
Field-Goal Percentage: Phegley, .477
Three-Point Percentage: Newlin, .296
Free-Throw Percentage: Newlin, .884
Scoring: Newlin, 20.9

Rebounds: Johnson, 602
Assists: Jordan, 557
Steals: Jordan, 223
Blocks: Johnson, 258

DRAFT CHOICES

1. Mike O'Koren	6-6	North Carolina
1a. Mike Gminski	6-11	Duke
3. Lowes Moore	6-2	West Va.
4. Rory Sparrow	6-2	Villanova
5. Aaron Curry	6-4	Oklahoma
6. Rick Mattick	7-0	LSU
7. Larry Spicer	6-8	Ala.-Birmingham
8. Lloyd Terry	6-10	New Orleans
9. Barry Young	6-5	Colorado St.
10. Rudy Macklin*	—	LSU

*Player not eligible.

ATLANTA HAWKS

Armond Hill

John Drew

Remember the days when they seemed to confuse the Atlanta Hawks with a rock group. "You lost to The Who?" No more. The Hawks are coming off their first division title since 1970. Their 50-32 record was a whopping nine games better than co-runners-up Houston and San Antonio. No more surprises. Everyone gets up for the Hawks these days.

Coach Hubie Brown's troops might have a slightly tougher time repeating in the revised Central Division which now includes super-power Milwaukee and Chicago in addition to holdovers Indiana, Cleveland, and Detroit.

But don't doubt that Hubie's boys will be ready. Atlanta plays hard-nosed basketball, led by all-pro 6-8 Dan Roundfield (16.5). The big question is co-captain 6-3 Eddie Johnson (18.5) who put in two straight years before running into police troubles over the summer. Johnson and 6-4 Armond Hill are Atlanta's floor leaders.

One-time hardship draftee 6-6 John Drew (19.5) slipped somewhat from his 22.0 ppg career mark. But he's still one of the league's top small forwards. 7-0 Tree Rollins (8.9) is one of the NBA's premier shot-rejectors and 6-9 Steve Hawes (9.3) continues to do a professional job. 6-11 Tom McMillen, a fine big forward sub (and sometime starter), is coming off a serious knee injury. (He missed 29 games in '80.)

Tiny 5-8 Charlie Criss (8.3), a three-year vet at age 31, continues to surprise. Late season addition 6-3 James McElroy suffered from assorted illnesses and injuries last year but should help at guard.

TEAM LEADERS — 1980

Minutes Played: Johnson, 2,622
Field-Goal Percentage: Rollins, .558
Three-Point Percentage: DNQ*
Free-Throw Percentage: Johnson, .828
Scoring: Drew, 19.5

Rebounds: Roundfield, 837
Steals: Johnson, 120
Assists: Hill, 424
Blocks: Rollins, 244

*No Hawk made the 25 3-pt. goals needed to qualify.

DRAFT CHOICES

1.	Don Collins	6-6	Washington State
2.	Craig Shelton	6-7	Georgetown
5.	Mike Doyle	6-4	South Carolina
6.	Mike Zagardo	6-10	George Washington
7.	Charles Hightower	6-6	Dillard (La.)
8.	Larry Lawrence*	—	Dartmouth
9.	Stan Lamb	6-2	Steubenville (Ohio)
10.	Mickey Dillard*	—	Florida St.

*Player not eligible.

MILWAUKEE BUCKS

Bob Lanier

Brian Winter

With the possible exception of L. A.'s Paul Westhead, there isn't a coach in the NBA who wouldn't swap problems with the Bucks' Don Nelson.

Milwaukee remains one of the youngest teams in the league, a team that plays hard every night—and not every one does. The only graybeard — 6-11 Bob Lanier who's 32—helped mold the team that went 49-33 in 1980 and won the division title. In 26 Milwaukee games, after coming over from Detroit, Bob averaged 15.7 ppg and grabbed off 6.9 rebounds. That's what Nelson was looking for.

You don't need much if you have 6-7 Marques Johnson (21.7) on your side. Milwaukee's version of a magic man led the team in just about every offensive department and was a shoo-in for all-pro honors.

Though 6-8 Dave Meyers (12.1) retired at age 27, the Bucks shouldn't miss him. Indiana's 6-10 Mickey Johnson is the replacement. 6-5 Junior Bridgeman could move in, bringing a 17.6 ppg average with him. Sharpshooting 6-4 Brian Winters (16.2) combines beautifully with quarterback and defensive ace 6-3 Quinn Buckner in the backcourt. 6-4 Sidney Moncrief (8.5) showed flashes of brilliance as a rookie. So did 6-9½ Pat Cummings (6.6), a hardnosed rebounder. 6-10 Rich Washington, hurting much of last season, is gone to Dallas in the expansion draft.

The college draft didn't provide much help for the Bucks, but not much was needed. The Bucks are ready to roll again.

TEAM LEADERS — 1980

Minutes Played: Johnson, 2,686
Field-Goal Percentage: Johnson, .544
Three-Point Percentage: Winters, .373
Free-Throw Percentage: Bridgeman, .865

Rebounds: Johnson, 566
Assists: Buckner, 383
Steals: Buckner, 135
Blocks: Catchings, 162

Scoring: Johnson, 21.7

DRAFT CHOICES

3.	Al Beal	6-9	Oklahoma
4.	Jeff Wolf	6-10	North Carolina
5.	Ken Jones	6-11	Va. Commonwealth
6.	Alex Gilbert	6-7	Indiana St.
7.	Ron White	6-2	Furman
8.	Keith Valentine	5-11	Va. Union
9.	Del Yarbrough	6-8	Illinois St.
10.	Malvin Crayton	6-7	Alabama St.

CHICAGO BULLS

David Greenwood

Reggie Theus

A healthy Artis Gilmore. That's the key to an improvement of Chicago's 30-52 record last year. The 7-2 giant who averaged 22.1 ppg in eight pro seasons before last year, missed 34 games and scored only 17.8 ppg in the 48 games he played in. Though top draftee 6-9 ½ David Greenwood picked up some of the slack with his 16.3 ppg scoring and his team-high 773 rebounds, it wasn't nearly enough.

Chicago's main man is Reggie Theus. The 6-7 Theus, the biggest guard in Bulls' history, did everything coach Jerry Sloan asked of him last year. He poured in 20.2 ppg (19th in the NBA), hit nearly 84% of his free throws, picked off 114 steals, and dished off a team-high 515 assists.

One of the Bulls' biggest off-season worries was at small forward. 6-7 Scott May, the one-time Indiana U. star, could be the man. He averaged 12.4 ppg in '80. But Scotty is the original hard luck guy. A pair of serious operations, a broken wrist, even a case of mononucleosis have all kept him out of the Bulls' line-up.

Sloan, starting his second season as the boss Bull with much more confidence, relies on several youngsters for extra depth. Ex-Iowa Hawkeye Ronnie Lester, who played all summer without his famous knee brace, should provide additional speed. And Marquette's Sam Worthen is a power player.

Chicago should be improved, but in the East's Central Division, it might not be enough.

TEAM LEADERS — 1980

Minutes Played: Theus, 3,029
Field-Goal Percentage: Gilmore, .595
Three-Point Percentage: Theus, .267
Free-Throw Percentage: Theus, .838
Scoring: Theus, 20.2

Rebounds: Greenwood, 773
Assists: Theus, 515
Steals: Sobers, 136
Blocks: Greenwood, 129

DRAFT CHOICES

1.	Kelvin Ransey*	6-1	Ohio St.
2.	Sam Worthen	6-5	Marquette
3.	James Wilkes	6-7	UCLA
4.	Ron Charles	6-7	Michigan St.
5.	Mike Campbell	6-10	Northwestern
6.	Bernard Rencher	6-2	St. John's
7.	Robert Byrd	6-6	Marquette
8.	Modzell Greer	6-6	North Park (Ill.)
9.	Jay Shidler	6-1	Kentucky
10.	Billy Foster	6-1	Eastern Montana

*Traded to Portland for Ronnie Lester.

INDIANA PACERS

James Edwards   Johnny Davis

It takes a basketball historian to remember when Slick Leonard was not the
Pacers' coach. (Actually, it was 1968.) Now
the Pacers have a pair of new leaders —
coach Jack McKinney and general manager Dick Vertlieb. Both are experienced
pros who should help the club.

But coaches and GMs don't score points,
so the two men have their work cut out for
them. They aren't without help, however.
There's 6-8 Mickey Johnson*, the 1980 Indiana scoring leader (19.1), who tailed off
after the deal which brought 6-8 one-time
super-pro George McGinnis back from
Denver. McGinnis, Indianapolis' favorite
son, slumped to 14.7 ppg (only 13.2 with
the Pacers), but is still a major threat when
he doesn't foul out (which he did 12 times
last season).

Johnny Davis, the Pacers' busiest man, led the team in assists (440) and free-throw percentage (86.4%) on top of his second-on-the-team 15.9 ppg scoring. Despite the presence of the four-year-vet, Indiana still spent the summer looking for a shooting guard.

7-0 James Edwards (15.7) is better than adequate at center and All-Rookie star Dudley Bradley (8.4) is a defensive whiz. Inconsistent 6-6 Billy Knight chipped in with 13.1 ppg and could help. So could draftees 6-8 Louis Orr and 6-3 Kenny Natt, brother of Portland All-Rookie Calvin.

*Traded to Milwaukee Bucks.

TEAM LEADERS — 1980

Minutes Played: Davis, 2,912
Field-Goal Percentage: Knight, .533
Three-Point Percentage: Hassett, .348
Free-Throw Percentage: J. Davis, .864

Rebounds: M. Johnson, 681*
Assists: J. Davis, 440
Steals: Bradley, 211
Blocks: C. Johnson, 121

Scoring: M. Johnson, 19.1

*George McGinnis totalled 699 rebounds for the season, 237 in 28 games for Indiana

DRAFT CHOICES

2.	Louis Orr	6-8	Syracuse
2a.	Kenny Natt	6-3	Northeast Louisiana
2b.	Dick Miller	6-6½	Toledo
4.	Rich Branning	6-3	Notre Dame
5.	Joe Galvin	7-0	Illinois St.
6.	Randy Owens	6-7	Phila. Textile
7.	Charles Naddaff	6-10	Lafayette
8.	Steve Stielper	6-8	James Madison (Va.)
9.	Scott Rogers	6-1	Kenyon (Ohio)
10.	John Bates	6-6	W. Va. Wesleyan

CLEVELAND CAVALIERS

Randy Smith

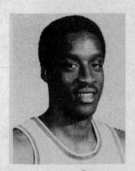

Kenny Carr

New Cav coach Bill Musselman knows a little something about defense. Once the small-college team he was coaching gave up an average of less than 34 points per game — over an entire season!

It's impossible for Stan Albeck's successor to repeat that feat with the pros. But the 1981 Cavaliers will play a hard-nosed game — or Musselman will know the reason why.

He starts with a team that plays decent defense anyway. The 1980 Cavs set a team record for steals (764), along with new marks for scoring (114.1, third in the league), and field-goal percentage (47.4%).

The loss of Austin Carr and his 11.8 ppg average to expansionist Dallas hurts the backcourt. But speedy Randy Smith is back with his 17.6 mark.

Big Dave Robisch, a free-agent most of the summer, surprised with his 15.3 mark. And 6-7, Bill Robinzine (11.4), the ex-King, replaces the traded (to N.Y.) Campy Russell.

Mike Mitchell is Musselman's ace in the hole. He played in all 82 games a year ago, poured in 22.2 ppg, grabbed 7.2 rebounds per outing, and was the key factor in Cleveland's 37-45 mark.

The jury is still out on Cleveland's draft picks. Musselman will have to get the most out of the available talent to keep his sanity.

TEAM LEADERS — 1980

Minutes Played: Mitchell, 2802
Field-Goal Percentage: Mitchell, .523
Three-Point Percentage: DNQ*
Free-Throw Percentage: Robisch, .842

Rebounds: Robisch, 658
Assists: Walker, 607
Steals: Walker, 155
Blocks: Mitchell, 77

Scoring: Mitchell, 22.2

*No Cavalier player made the 25 3-pt. goals needed to qualify.

DRAFT CHOICES

1.	Chad Kinch	6-4	No. Carolina-Charlotte
3.	Stuart House	6-11	Washington St.
3a.	Wayne Abrams	6-6	So. Illinois
3b.	Ron Jones	6-4	Illinois St.
5.	Lavon Williams	6-6	Kentucky
6.	Antonio Martin	6-8	Oral Roberts
7.	Leroy Berry	6-3	Wilmington (Ohio)
8.	Jim Ellinghausen	6-8	Ohio St.
9.	Melvin Crafter	6-5	Central St. (Ohio)
10.	PASS		

DETROIT PISTONS

Terry Tyler

Bob McAdoo

When your team wins only 16 games and loses 66, there's only one way to go and that's up. Scotty Robertson, the Pistons' new coach (who replaced Richie Adubato who replaced Dick Vitale who replaced...), has a team of solid starters with lots of question marks behind them.

Six-ten Bob McAdoo, one of the NBA's top scoring machines ever, "slumped" to 21.1 ppg last year, his lowest output since 1973, his rookie year. The small forward opposite McAdoo is 6-5 John Long who continued to blossom as an NBA sophomore last season. John, who poured in 16.1 ppg as a rookie improved to 19.4 as a second-year man while continuing to improve in every phase of his game.

56

Burly 6-11 Kent Benson figures to anchor the middle for Robertson & Co. The ex-Indiana ace who once was the Bucks' top choice in the NBA draft, came to Detroit for all-timer Bob Lanier. He showed enough in 17 Piston games to earn the starting berth for 1981.

Overall, the Pistons lost some 185 player-games to injury in 1980. Improved health — as well as improvement by youngsters like 6-8 Phil Hubbard (9.1), 6-7 Greg Kelser (14.2 but only 50 games), and 6-7 Terry Tyler (12.3)—is a key to Detroit's 1981 season. Detroit also needs help at the point guard position.

TEAM LEADERS — 1980

Minutes Played: Tyler, 2,670
Field-Goal Percentage: Long, .505
Three-Point Percentage: DNQ*
Free-Throw Percentage: Long, .825

Rebounds: Tyler, 627
Assists: Money, 254
Steals: Long, 129
Blocks: Tyler, 220

Scoring: Tyler, 12.3[a]

*No Piston made the 25 3-point goals needed to qualify.
[a]McAdoo, Long, and Kelser each outscored Tyler but did not qualify on total games or total points.

DRAFT CHOICES

1.	Larry Drew	6-1	Missouri
2.	Brad Branson	6-10	SMU
3.	Jonathan Moore	6-8	Furman
4.	Darwin Cook	6-3	Portland
5.	Tony Fuller	6-4	Pepperdine
6.	Tony Turner	6-5	Alaska-Anchor age
7.	Carl Pierce	6-7	Gonzaga
8.	Leroy Loggins	6-6	Fairmont St. (W. Va.)
9.	Terry Dupris	6-1	Huron (S.D.)
10.	Steve Johnson*	—	Oregon St.

*Player not eligible

KANSAS CITY KINGS

Phil Ford

Scott Wedman

The Kings are not at all unhappy to say good-bye to the Milwaukee Bucks, the 1980 Midwest champs, now located in the Central Division.

Kansas City and coach Cotton Fitzsimmons enjoyed the summer, knowing that their starters were set. It's a group that combines size and speed with youth and experience. The backcourt is one of the best in the business with tricky 6-2 Phil Ford and 6-4 shooting star Otis Birdsong. Ford, the ex-North Carolina and Olympic champ, is an absolute magician with the ball, tossing off 610 assists (6th in the NBA) and 16.2 ppg (despite a late-season slump). At 6-4 Birdsong was the NBA's No. 9 scorer (22.7), a feat he thanks Ford for. Together, they work perfectly.

Burly 6-10 Sam Lacey starts his 11th NBA season as the Kings' No. 1 center. Though

Sam's numbers (9.2 ppg, 645 rebounds) have been better, he remains the Kings' team leader.

Second-year man 6-6 Reggie King and 6-7 Scott Wedman, now in his seventh year, are the forwards. King enjoyed a brilliant rookie campaign, starting 44 of 82 games, scoring 8.2 ppg, and grabbing 6.9 rebounds per game, second to Lacey among the Kings. Wedman, a solid player year in and year out, had a career-high 19.0 ppg.

Kaycee's biggest needs? A back-up point guard: hopefully new King Jo Jo White. A back-up center: hopefully 6-10 ex-Piston Leon Douglas. A swing guard-forward: hopefully top draftee Hawkeye Whitney of N. C. State.

TEAM LEADERS — 1980

Minutes Played: Birdsong, 2,885
Field-Goal Percentage: King, .515
Three-Point Percentage: DNQ*
Free-Throw Percentage: Ford, .818

Rebounds: King, 566
Assists: Ford, 610
Steals: Birdsong, Ford, 136
Blocks: Lacey, 109

Scoring: Birdsong, 22.7

*No King made the 25 3-pt. goals needed to qualify.

DRAFT CHOICES

1.	Hawkeye Whitney	6-5	N.C. State
3.	Tony Murphy	6-2	Southern U. (La.)
5.	Kelvin Blakely	6-7	Eastern Michigan
6.	Trent Grooms	6-7	Kent St.
7.	Arnold McDowell	6-4	Montana St.
8.	Kevin Singleton*	—	California
9.	Charles Cole	6-1	Delta St. (Miss.)
10.	Johnny Nash*	—	Arizona St.

*Player not eligible

Midwest Division
SAN ANTONIO SPURS

James Silas

Mark Olberding

In San Antonio, where George Gervin has replaced the Alamo as the No. 1 local attraction, new coach Stan Albeck is priming his club for a run at the division title. The ex-Cleveland bench boss (37-45 with the 1980 Cavs) searched desperately for a center all summer, but could do no better than Net middle man 6-11 George Johnson.

With Gervin pouring in points with Texas type regularity, Johnson may be enough. The 6-7 Iceman is a point-making machine (his all-time best 33.1 ppg scoring won him a third-straight NBA point title). 6-9 Larry Kenon, unhappy during

60

much of the off-season (money, as usual) is an impressive rebounder (9.9 per game) and scorer (20.1). But he won't be back.

6-3 James Silas seems to be healthy again, a big plus for coach Albeck. James tossed in 20 or more points during 23 of the Spurs' last 39 1980 contests. Inconsistent 6-9 John Shumate scored only 8.9 ppg last year, but had 14.5 in 27 Spurs contests and is still a powerhouse inside. 6-10 Kevin Restani, the ex-Buck, was adequate (10.7). 6-4 Mike Gale (6.6) has lost a step at age 30.

Powerful 6-9 Reggie Johnson of Tennessee, the Spurs' first-round draft pick, figures to get lots of playing time.

TEAM LEADERS — 1980

Minutes Played: Gervin, 2,934
Field-Goal Percentage: Gervin, .528
Three-Point Percentage: Gervin, .314
Free-Throw Percentage: Silas, .887

Rebounds: Kenon, 775
Assists: Silas, 347
Steals: Gale, 123
Blocks: Gervin, 79

Scoring: Gervin, 33.1

DRAFT CHOICES

1.	Reggie Johnson	6-9	Tennessee
2.	Michael Wiley	6-8	Long Beach St.
3.	Lavon Mercer	6-9½	Georgia
3a.	Rich Yonakor	6-9	North Carolina
4.	Calvin Roberts	6-7	Cal. St.-Fullerton
5.	Gib Hinz	7-0	Wisc.-Eau Claire
6.	Dean Uthoff	6-11	Iowa St.
7.	Alan Zahn	6-7	Arkansas
8.	Bill Bailey	6-2	Pan American
9.	Al Williams	6-8	No. Texas St.
10.	Steve Schall	6-11	Arkansas

HOUSTON ROCKETS

Calvin Murphy

Allen Leavell

The Rockets hope their team doctor has an easy year in 1981. He was the busiest man on the Houston roster last season, as the Rockets lost 100 player games to injury. (When three players miss a game due to injury, that counts as three player-games.)

Only Moses Malone and Major Jones were spared the injury bug. And if you can only have a couple of healthy players, the 6-10 Malone is as good a choice as anyone. The all-pro led the Rockets in just about every offensive department (except assists and steals).

When he's right, 6-8 Rudy T. (for Tomjanovich) is one tough customer. He scored 14.2 ppg (for the 62 games he played in), while pulling down 5.8 rebounds per outing, tied with 6-8 Robert Reid (13.0) for second high on the team.

The backcourt, with vets like tiny (5-10 or less) Calvin Murphy (20.0, 143 steals) and 6-3 Tom Henderson (5.5) and top rookie 6-1 Allen Leavell (10.9 and a team-leading 5.4 assists per game), is solid. 6-8 Rick Barry (12.0), at age 36, is gone, taking with him the league's best foul-shooting mark (93.5%) and a 33% mark on three-point goals. But Houston could have a sleeper replacement in 6-11 Lee Johnson, the Rockets' No. 1 draft pick in 1979. Johnson, who flopped at Houston's pre-season camp a year ago, spent a year in Italy and came back stronger and better than ever.

In their realigned division, Houston is counting on 48 wins and a possible division title.

TEAM LEADERS — 1980

Minutes Played: Malone, 3,140
Field-Goal Percentage: Leavell, .503
Three-Point Percentage: Barry, .330
Free-Throw Percentage: Barry, .935
Rebounds: Malone, 1,190
Assists: Leavell, 417
Steals: Murphy, 143
Blocks: Malone, 107
Scoring: Malone, 25.8

DRAFT CHOICES

2.	John Stroud	6-6	Mississippi
2a.	Terry Stotts	6-8	Oklahoma
2b.	Billy Williams	6-4	Clemson
4.	Dean Hunger	6-8	Utah St.
5.	Slab Jones	6-8	New Mexico St.
6.	Everette Jefferson	6-6	New Mexico
7.	Joe Nehls	6-4	Arizona
8.	Rosie Barnes	6-3	Bowling Green
9.	PASS		
10.	Ed Turner*	—	Texas A&I

*Player not eligible

Midwest Division
DENVER NUGGETS

Dan Issel

David Thompson

The most optimistic Nugget fan is the lady who answers the team's phone. "Rebound '80" is the greeting a caller receives. That was the Nuggets' goal as they prepared for the current season.

"We want to get off to a quick start," says Coach Donnie Walsh. "We got our players in early (around August 1), had them running, working on Nautilus machines, preparing for the opening bell. And the rookies and free agents checked in by August 15."

The key to a quick start — and an improvement on last year's 30-52 record — was the return to health by Denver's own Mr. Skywalker, 6-4 David Thompson. After missing 43 games a year ago, D.T. came back in super shape, insisting that he was jumping better than ever. If that's true, the Midwest Division is in for a tough time.

At age 32, 6-9 Dan Issel hasn't lost a thing. He tossed in 23.8 ppg a year ago, seventh in the league. He also hit 50.5% of his shots, grabbed 719 rebounds, pulled off 88 steals, and even blocked 54 shots. Not bad for an old man. Top choice 6-9 James Ray can fill in for Issel.

6-3 John Roche, re-signed just before training camp, is one of the top point-guard candidates, along with free agent Ken Higgs and ex-Blazer T.R. Dunn.

But Walsh isn't too worried about the point guard spot. "We're going to full-court press all game and run every time we get the ball. With that style of play, we may not be setting up that often."

TEAM LEADERS — 1980

Minutes Played: Issel, 2,938
Field-Goal Percentage: Issel, .505
Three-Point Percentage: Roche, .380
Free-Throw Percentage: Roche, .866
Rebounds: Issel, 719
Assists: Roche, 405
Steals: Wilkerson, 93
Blocks: Hughes, 77
Scoring: Issel, 23.8

DRAFT CHOICES

1.	James Ray	6-9	Jacksonville
1a.	Carl Nicks	6-2½	Indiana St.
2.	Jawann Oldham	7-0	Seattle
3.	Kurt Nimphius	6-10	Arizona St.
3a.	Eddie Lee	6-4	Cincinnati
3b.	Ronnie Valentine	6-7	Old Dominion
4.	Sammie Ellis	6-6½	Pittsburgh
5.	James Patrick	6-5	SW Texas St.
6.	Ernie Hill	6-4	Oklahoma City
7.	Tommy Springer	6-0	Vanderbilt
8.	Frank Johnson*	—	Wake Forest
9.	Jim Graziano	6-9	So. Carolina
10.	Earl Sango	6-7	Regis (Col.)

*Player not eligible.

UTAH JAZZ

Allan Bristow

Adrian Dantley

There's nothing wrong with the Utah Jazz that Kareem Abdul-Jabbar and Phil Ford wouldn't help. But since the Lakers and Kings are unlikely to part with their stars, the Jazz will have to make do with the talent on hand.

Coach Tom Nissalke has one proven pro in 6-5 Adrian Dantley. The well-traveled ex-Notre Dame star, now playing at a slim 205 pounds, scored 28.0 ppg last year, third in the NBA behind George Gervin and Lloyd Free. He also was the top rebounder (516 in 68 games) among the 20 players who wore a Jazz uniform in 1980.

The death of Terry Furlow, who scored 16.0 ppg for Utah last year, robs the club of a budding star. Jazz fans were counting on the return of 6-7 Bernard King, the talented but troubled star who played in only 19 games a year ago. But Utah dealt him to Golden State for Wayne Cooper and a 1981 draft choice.

The Jazz' major weakness last season was at guard. General manager Frank Layden thinks the team's draft will fill those two holes. Though neither player was signed when the team went to camp, both 6-4 jumping jack Darrell Griffith of Louisville and 6-3½ John Duren of Georgetown could serve as Utah's big guard and point guard for the next 10 years. (The sight of Griffith *hurdling* the high-jump bar at the TV Superstars' obstacle course is awesome.)

To eliminate the possibility of repeating last year's player shuttle, Utah took only 11 players to this year's training camp. If they were the right players, look for the Jazz to add eight or nine wins to their 24-58 1980 total.

TEAM LEADERS—1980

Minutes Played: Dantley, 2,674
Field-Goal Percentage: Dantley, .576
Three-Point Percentage: DNQ*
Free-Throw Percentage: Boone, .893
Scoring: Dantley, 28.0

Rebounds: Poquette, 560
Assists: Bristow, 341
Steals: Williams, 100
Blocks: Poquette, 162

*No Jazz player made the 25 3-pt. goals needed to qualify.

DRAFT CHOICES

1.	Darrell Griffith	6-4	Louisville
1a.	John Duren	6-3½	Georgetown
4.	Alan Taylor	6-10	Brigham Young
5.	Wally West	6-9	Boston U.
6.	Ken Cunningham	6-2	Western Mich.
7.	Dave Colescott	6-1	North Carolina
8.	Jim Brandon	6-5	St. Peter's
9.	Paul Renfro	6-9	Texas-Arlington
10.	Leroy Coleman	6-4	Middle Tennessee

DALLAS MAVERICKS

Tom LaGarde   Dick Motta

Would you believe the Dallas Mavericks were caught in a giant argument before they played their first game? Believe it. When the NBA's newest basketball team chose its nickname, the Mavericks, the nearby U. of Texas at Arlington, just a few miles down the turnpike, screamed. Seems that their teams are called Mavericks too.

For new coach Dick Motta, there are more important things to worry about than nicknames. First, the veteran coach (Bulls, Bullets) must figure out how to win games with a bunch of players their old teams didn't want.

Actually, he has a better chance than some other expansion coaches. There are some talented players on the Mavs' roster, including a pretty beefy front-line.

6-10, 230-pound Tom LaGarde, a some-time Seattle starter, gets another chance in Texas. He has never really bounced back from a torn knee ligament in 1978.

If 6-11 Rich Washington recovers from off-season surgery, he'll really help. An all-rookie star with the Kings in 1977, he should improve on his 5.9 ppg average with the Bucks in 1980.

Dallas also got front-court help in the free-agent and draft departments. Former UCLA star 7-2 Ralph Drollinger turns pro after four years with the amateur Athletes in Action team. And another UCLA ace, 6-8 Kiki Vandeweghe, would be the solid strong forward Motta needs. But Kiki, who averaged 19.5 ppg for the Bruins' national runners-up last year, made it clear that he wasn't thrilled about going to Dallas.

DRAFT CHOICES

1. Kiki Vandeweghe	6-8	UCLA
2. Roosevelt Bouie	6-11	Syracuse
3. David Britton	6-4	Texas A&M
4. David Johnson	6-8	Weber St.
5. Darrell Allums	6-8	UCLA
6. Leroy Jackson	6-3	Cameron (Okla.)
7. Tony Forch	6-5	Midwestern St. (Texas)
8. Clarence Kea	6-7	Lamar
9. Juice Williams	6-1	Houston
10. Tom Morgan	6-6	Cal. St.-Fullerton

LOS ANGELES LAKERS

Jamaal Wilkes

Norm Nixon

When you're on top, everyone guns for you. Still, it's a lot of fun to be the top dog—and the Lakers were "best-in-show" last season. Their goal for 1981: to become the first NBA team since the 1968 and '69 Boston Celtics to win two straight NBA titles.

The ingredients are there. Kareem Abdul-Jabbar, at age 33, was never better that he was last season. The 7-2 (or more) giant poured through 24.8 ppg, sixth best in the NBA, was the top shot blocker (3.41 average), was eighth in rebounding (10.8 per game), and won another league MVP award. The best big-man ever? Probably.

At 6-9 Magic Johnson had a rookie year that would make a great show for TV's "That's Incredible." Averaging 36.3 minutes per outing, Magic hit 53% of his field goal tries, 81% of his foul shots, grabbed 596 rebounds from his guard spot (a 7.7 average), dished off 7.3 assists per game (seventh in the league), pulled off 2.43

steals per contest, and won the final playoff game just about single-handedly with 42 points, his biggest game ever.

Though the team cut loose 6-9 Spencer Haywood and his 9.7 ppg, there's plenty of help with 6-9 Jamaal Wilkes (20.0), one of the league's top small forwards, ball-handling 6-2 Norm Nixon (17.6 ppg, 642 assists), and 6-11 Jim Chones (10.6, 6.9 rebounds per game). Second-year man 6-6 Mike Cooper (8.8) would have been the top rookie on any team that didn't have Magic Johnson. L.A. picked up Dr. Dunk, Darnell Hillman, just before training camp to help fill Haywood's spot.

TEAM LEADERS — 1980

Minutes Played: Abdul-Jabbar, 3,143

Field-Goal Percentage: Abdul-Jabbar, .604

Three-Point Percentage: DNQ*

Free-Throw Percentage: Johnson, .810

Rebounds: Abdul-Jabbar, 886

Assists: Nixon, 642

Steals: Johnson, 187

Blocks: Abdul-Jabbar, 280

Scoring: Abdul-Jabbar, 24.8

*No Laker made the 25 3-pt. goals needed to qualify.

DRAFT CHOICES

2.	Wayne Robinson	6-9	Virginia Tech
2a.	Butch Carter	6-5	Indiana
4.	Tony Jackson	6-0	Florida St.
4a.	Ron Baxter	6-4	Texas
5.	Rick Raivio	6-5	Portland
6.	Odis Boddie	6-2	No. Alabama
7.	Charles Davis*	—	Vanderbilt
8.	Melvin Hooker	6-8	Edinboro (Pa.) St.
9.	PASS		
10.	PASS		

*Player not eligible.

Pacific Division
SEATTLE SUPERSONICS

Jack Sikma

Lonnie Shelton

The Dennis Johnson for Paul Westphal trade may hold the key to Seattle's 1981 success. Sonics' coach Len Wilkens, armed with a new two-year contract, should get more offense from Westphal than he did from Johnson. But how much will the loss of DJ's defense hurt? And how will Paul blend with his new backcourt partner, Gus Williams?

A couple of off-season departures hurt Seattle. Back-up forward Paul Silas (38) went from one of the league's oldest players to its youngest coach (San Diego). Backup center Tom LaGarde (4.7, 3.8 rebounds) was lost to Dallas.

But the remaining cast is solid. Speedy 6-2 Williams was never better than last year, leading the team in minutes, shots (tried and made), steals, points, and average (22.1). At 6-11, Jack Sikma (14.3) is a tremendous threat under the boards and his 11.1 rebounds per game led the team. He could be the key to Seattle's 1981 hopes.

Dennis Johnson's departure leaves 6-7 John Johnson (11.3) as the team's No. 1 Johnson. John was the team's leader in assists a year ago, but he also led in turnovers (247). Downtown Freddy Brown tossed in 12 ppg, his lowest average ever, but hit 44.3%, tops in the league, on his three-point shots, only a couple of percents lower than his two-point mark (47.9%). That's sharp shooting!

Rugged 6-8 Lonnie Shelton is the Sonics' best shooter 53%) and offensive rebounder, though he's too prone to foul. And former Rutgers star 6-9 James Bailey (4.7) impressed with his shot-blocking and ball-stuffing ability as a rookie.

TEAM LEADERS — 1980

Minutes Played: Williams, 2,969
Field-Goal Percentage: Shelton, .530
Three-Point Percentage: Brown, .443
Free-Throw Percentage: Brown, .837
Rebounds: Sikma, 908
Assists: J. Johnson, 424
Steals: Williams, 200
Blocks: D. Johnson, 82
Scoring: Williams, 22.1

DRAFT CHOICES

1.	Bill Hanzlik	6-6	Notre Dame
3.	Carl Bailey	7-0	Tuskegee (Ala.)
4.	Gary Hooker	6-5½	Murray (Ky.) St.
5.	Lenny Horton	6-7	Ga. Tech
6.	Jim Strickland	6-10	So. Carolina
7.	Cal Ervin	6-1	Seattle
8.	Al Dutch	6-7	Georgetown
9.	Jim Tillman	6-4	Eastern Ky.
10.	Kent Williams	6-4	Texas Tech

PHOENIX SUNS

Truck Robinson

Alvan Adams

The Suns' only problem is geography. The team's 55-27 record, third in the Pacific Division, was good enough to win either the Central or Midwest races, with room to spare.

Sadly for Phoenix, Arizona is still located near the western ocean, and the division rivals still wear shirts marked Lakers, Sonics, and Blazers.

Coach John MacLeod thinks he's well-equipped for another run at a division (and NBA) title. True, All-Pro Paul Westphal (21.9) is gone to Seattle. But the new kid in town, Seattle's Dennis (D. J.) Johnson, could actually contribute more. He averaged 19.0 for the Sonics last season, tossed off 332 assists, made 144 steals, and even blocked 82 shots. He's a shoo-in for the NBA's All-Defensive team.

The rest of the Suns' starters have been All-Stars at least once during their careers. Hefty (6-7, 239-pounds) Truck Robinson is many coaches' idea of what a power forward should be. His 17.3 ppg average meshes neatly with the 21.5 (15th in the league) by small forward 6-6 All-Pro Walter Davis. Robinson was the team's top rebounder (9.4 per game); Davis was second in scoring, assists (4.5), and steals.

Injury-prone 6-9 Alvan Adams should be at center again, after his best shooting season (53.1%) and scored 14.9 ppg after missing six early games with a foot problem. Vet 6-4 Don Buse (7.7) should join Johnson in the backcourt, if off-season foot ills don't hamper him.

TEAM LEADERS — 1980

Minutes Played: Robinson, 2,710
Field-Goal Percentage: Davis, .563
Three-Point Percentage: Westphal, .280
Free-Throw Percentage: Bratz, .870

Rebounds: Robinson, 770
Assists: Westphal, 416
Steals: Buse, 132
Blocks: Robinson, 59*

Scoring: Westphal, 21.9

*Kelley had 96 blocks in 1980, including 17 in 23 Suns' games.

DRAFT CHOICES

2.	Kim Belton	6-6½	Stanford
3.	John Campbell	6-9	Clemson
3a.	Doug True	6-8	California
4.	Leroy Stampley	6-2	Loyola (Ill.)
5.	Mark Stevens	6-6	Northern Arizona
6.	Coby Leavitt	6-9	Utah
7.	Ron Williams	6-4	Western Montana
8.	Mo Connolly	6-7	LaSalle
9.	Keith French	6-7	North Park (Ill.)
10.	Randy Carroll	6-5	Kansas

PORTLAND TRAIL BLAZERS

Tom Owens

Ron Brewer

A 38-44 record, though good enough for a playoff spot, isn't good enough for Jack Ramsay and his Blazers. Though Portland is one of the most solid and best-coached teams in the NBA every year, something was missing in '80. A check of the league stats may indicate the reason. Only Kermit Washington (ninth in rebounding, eighth in shooting) managed to crack the Top Ten in anything.

The 6-8 Washington (13.4), who came to Portland from San Diego when Bill Walton went south, did a bang-up job for the Blazers. He pulled down 842 rebounds (102.2 per game), 325 off the offensive boards.

So can Calvin Natt, the ex-Net, who burned up the cords in his rookie year, with a 19.9 ppg scoring mark, 691 rebounds, 102 steals, and more. Portland parted with Maurice Lucas and two No. 1

draft picks but Natt is worth it. Just when you think Portland can't win with Tom Owens at center, the 6-10 South Carolina grad surprises, though his 1980 numbers didn't match his '79 totals. The return of 6-10 Mychal Thompson, out all last year after a biking accident, will really help.

6-4 Ron Brewer is a classy guard who does everything well. The second-year-man averaged 15.7 ppg, up from 13.3 as a rookie. Surprising 6-1 Dave Twardzik was Portland's assist leader but only an 8.5 scorer. Rookie Abdul-Jeelani is gone to Dallas after a 9.8 ppg first season.

TEAM LEADERS — 1980

Minutes Played: R. Brewer, 2,815
Field-Goal Percentage: Washington, .553
Three-Point Percentage: DNQ*
Free-Throw Percentage: R. Brewer, .840

Rebounds: Washington, 842
Assists: Twardzik, 273
Steals: Dunn, 102
Blocks: Washington, 131

Scoring: Owens, 16.4[a]

*No Blazer player made the 25 3-pt. goals needed to qualify.
[a]Natt averaged 19.8 ppg, including 20.4 in 32 games with Portland.

DRAFT CHOICES

1.	Ronnie Lester*	6-1½	Iowa
2.	David Lawrence	6-8½	McNeese St. (La.)
2a.	Bruce Collins	6-5	Weber St.
3.	Michael Harper	6-10	North Park (Ill.)
4.	Kelvin Henderson	6-7	St. Louis
5.	Larry Belin	6-8	New Mexico
6.	Perry Mirkovich	6-6½	Lethbridge (Canada)
7.	Gig Sims	6-9	UCLA
8.	John Stroeder	6-10	Montana
9.	Rick Boucher	6-3	Maine
10.	Dave Kuffeld	6-8	Yeshiva

*Traded to Chicago for Kelvin Ransey.

SAN DIEGO CLIPPERS

Swen Nater

Freeman Williams

Paul Silas, one of the world's oldest power forwards a year ago, becomes the NBA's youngest head coach with San Diego. The job won't be easy — but Silas doesn't know the easy way.

He has some help, of course. The brilliant offensive machine, Lloyd (All-World) Free was the league's No. 2 scorer last year. His 30.2 ppg average trailed only George Gervin (33.1). But Lloyd can find ways to hurt his own team, too, and always seems on the verge of being traded. (And he was, to Golden State, at press time.)

In the absence of Bill Walton, out for all but 14 games, Swen Nater (13.4) became the league's top rebounder, averaging 15 recoveries per game. Swen isn't the most talented player, but on a missed shot he's often the smartest. He set San Diego records for total rebounds (1,216), offensive rebounds (352), and defensive rebounds (864).

Freeman Williams was a pleasant surprise for the two-year-old franchise. He poured in 18.6 ppg, including one 51-point outburst, best on the team. Brian Taylor, Free's backcourt partner, also surprised with his 13.5 ppg scoring and his team-leading 335 assists.

Depth—San Diego doesn't have much—is an on-going problem. Hopefully, draftees like Michael Brooks of LaSalle, one of the big names of the Southern California summer pro league, will help. San Diego didn't miss the playoffs by much last year (three games behind Portland). But the Clippers are hampered by playing in the league's toughest division.

TEAM LEADERS — 1980

Minutes Played: Nater, 2,860
Field-Goal Percentage: Nater, .554
Three-Point Percentage: Taylor, .377
Free-Throw Percentage: Williams, .815
Rebounds: Nater, 1,216
Assists: Taylor, 335
Steals: Taylor, 147
Blocks: Wicks, 52
Scoring: Free, 30.2

DRAFT CHOICES

1.	Michael Brooks	6-7	LaSalle
4.	Ed Odom	6-3	Oklahoma St.
5.	Wally Rank	6-6½	San Jose St.
6.	Londale Theus	6-3	Santa Clara
7.	Paul Anderson	6-3	So. Calif. College
8.	PASS		
9.	PASS		
10.	PASS		

GOLDEN STATE WARRIORS

Lloyd Free   Bernard King

How sad! The 1975 NBA champions sank into the Pacific (division, that is) in 1980. The Warriors' 24-58 mark, tied for second worst in the league, placed them 36 games behind the top-dog Lakers and 11 games behind fifth-place San Diego. The '81 outlook isn't much better, either.

Golden State got its man in the June draft, Purdue's seven-footer Joe Barry Carroll. Most scouts agree that he could be a star of the future. But the price was dear: the Warriors gave up their top shooter and rebounder, Robert Parish, along with their No. 1 draft pick. (Boston picked Minnesota's Kevin McHale as part of the deal.)

Joe Barry joins a tattered crew, led by top-scorer 6-7 forward Purvis Short (17.0), who missed the last 16 games in '80 with a shoulder separation.

Last-minute additions, like Lloyd (All-World) Free (from San Diego) and Bernard

King (from Utah) will provide much needed firepower. John Lucas is still one of the league's best assist men (7.5 per game, fifth in the NBA), but his scoring slipped to 12.6 per outing. He also missed two games (flu), ending a streak of 317 straight. 6-7 Sonny Parker, who started every Warrior game, led the team in a variety of offensive departments, but shot only 39.7% during the last 13 games.

If Carroll doesn't make it immediately, 6-9 Cliff Ray, an eight-year vet, will have to do the job. Ray, who will be 32 in January, was limited to six points per game depite averaging 20.8 minutes.

TEAM LEADERS — 1980

Minutes Played: Parker, 2,849
Field-Goal Percentage: Parish, .507
Three-Point Percentage: DNQ*
Free-Throw Percentage: Short, .812

Rebounds: Parish, 783
Assists: Lucas, 602
Steals: Parker, 173
Blocks: Parisy, 115

Scoring: Short, 17.0

*No Warrior player made the 25 3-pt. goals needed to qualify.

DRAFT CHOICES

1.	Joe Barry Carroll	7-0	Purdue
1a.	Rickey Brown	6-10	Mississippi St.
2.	Larry Smith	6-8	Alcorn St. (Miss.)
2a.	Jeff Ruland*	6-9	Iona
3.	John Virgil	6-4	North Carolina
4.	Robert Scott	6-1	Alabama
5.	Don Carfino	6-2	USC
6.	Neil Bresnahan	6-6	Illinois
7.	Lorenzo Romar	6-1	Washington
8.	Kurt Kanaskie	6-1	LaSalle
9.	Billy Reid	6-5	San Francisco
10.	Tim Higgins	6-5	Kearney St. (Neb.)

*Traded to Washington for future considerations.

1979-80
N.B.A. STANDINGS

EASTERN CONFERENCE

Atlantic Division	W	L	Pct.	GB
Boston	61	21	.744	--
Philadelphia	59	23	.720	2
Washington	39	43	.476	22
New York	39	43	.476	22
New Jersey	34	48	.415	27

Central Division				
Atlanta	50	32	.610	--
Houston	41	41	.500	9
San Antonio	41	41	.500	9
Indiana	37	45	.451	13
Cleveland	37	45	.451	13
Detroit	16	66	.195	34

WESTERN CONFERENCE

Midwest Division				
Milwaukee	49	33	.598	--
Kansas City	47	35	.573	2
Denver	30	52	.366	19
Chicago	30	52	.366	19
Utah	24	58	.293	25

Pacific Division				
Los Angeles	60	22	.732	--
Seattle	56	26	.683	4
Phoenix	55	27	.671	5
Portland	38	44	.463	22
San Diego	35	47	.427	25
Golden State	24	58	.293	36

1979-80 STATISTICS

George Gervin

INDIVIDUAL SCORING

Minimum: 70 games played or 1,400 points

	G	FG	FT	PTS.	AVG.
Gervin, S.A.	78	1024	505	2585	33.1
Free, S.D.	68	737	572	2055	30.2
Dantley, Utah	68	730	443	1903	28.0
Erving, Phil.	78	838	420	2100	26.9
Malone, Hou.	82	778	563	2119	25.8
Abdul-Jabbar, L.A.	82	835	364	2034	24.8
Issel, Den.	82	715	517	1951	23.8
Hayes, Wash.	81	761	334	1859	23.0
Birdsong, K.C.	82	781	286	1858	22.7
Mitchell, Clev.	82	775	270	1820	22.2
G. Williams, Sea.	82	739	331	1816	22.1
Westphal, Phoe.	82	692	382	1792	21.9
Cartwright, N.Y.	82	665	451	1781	21.7
Johnson, Mil.	77	689	291	1671	21.7
Davis, Phoe.	75	657	299	1613	21.5
Bird, Bos.	82	693	301	1745	21.3
Newlin, N.J.	78	611	367	1634	20.9
R. Williams, N.Y.	82	687	333	1714	20.9
Theus, Chi.	82	566	500	1660	20.2
Kenon, S.A.	78	647	270	1565	20.1

FIELD GOALS

Minimum: 300 Made

	FG	FGA	PCT.
Maxwell, Bos.	457	750	.609
Abdul-Jabbar, L.A.	835	1383	.604
Gilmore, Chi.	305	513	.595
Dantley, Utah	730	1267	.576
Boswell, Utah	346	613	.564
Davis, Phoe.	657	1166	.563
Nater, S.D.	443	799	.554
Washington, Port.	421	761	.553
Cartwright, N.Y.	665	1215	.547
Johnson, Mil.	689	1267	.544

Cedric Maxwell

FREE THROW LEADERS

Minimum: 125 Made

	FT	FTA	PCT.
Barry, Hou.	143	153	.935
Murphy, Hou.	271	302	.897
Boone, Utah	175	196	.893
Silas, S.A.	339	382	.887
Newlin, N.J.	367	415	.884
Furlow, Utah	171	196	.872
Phegley, N.J.	177	203	.872
Bratz, Phoe.	141	162	.870
Grevey, Wash.	216	249	.867
Roche, Den.	175	202	.866

Rick Barry

ASSISTS

Minimum: 70 games or 400 assists

	G	NO.	AVG.
Richardson, N.Y.	82	832	10.1
Archibald, Bos.	80	671	8.4
Walker, Clev.	76	607	8.0
Nixon, L.A.	82	642	7.8
Lucas, G.S.	80	602	7.5
Ford, K.C.	82	610	7.4
Johnson, L.A.	77	563	7.3
Cheeks, Phil.	79	556	7.0
Jordan, N.J.	82	557	6.8
Porter, Wash.	70	457	6.5

M.R. Richardson

BLOCKED SHOTS

Minimum: 70 games or 100 blocked shots

	G	NO.	AVG.
Abdul-Jabbar, L.A.	82	280	3.41
Johnson, N.J.	81	258	3.19
Rollins, Atl.	82	244	2.98
Tyler, Det.	82	220	2.68
Hayes, Wash.	81	189	2.33
Catchings, Mil.	72	162	2.25
C. Jones, Phil	80	162	2.03
Poquette, Utah	82	162	1.98
Meriweather, N.Y.	65	120	1.85
Erving, Phil.	78	140	1.79

Kareem Abdul-Jabbar

STEALS

Minimum: 70 games or 125 steals

	G	NO.	AVG.
Richardson, N.Y.	82	265	3.23
Jordan, N.J.	82	223	2.72
Bradley, Ind.	82	211	2.57
Williams, Sea.	82	200	2.44
Johnson, L.A.	77	187	2.43
Cheeks, Phil.	79	183	2.32
Erving, Phil.	78	170	2.18
Parker, G.S.	82	173	2.11
Walker, Clev.	76	155	2.04
R. Williams, N.Y.	82	167	2.04

M.R. Richardson

REBOUNDS

Minimum: 70 games or 800 rebounds

	G	OFF	DEF	TOT	AVG.
Nater, S.D.	81	352	864	1216	15.0
Malone, Hou.	82	573	617	1190	14.5
Unseld, Wash.	82	334	760	1094	13.3
C. Jones, Phil.	80	219	731	950	11.9
Sikma, Sea.	82	198	710	908	11.1
Hayes, Wash.	81	269	627	896	11.1
Parish, G.S.	72	247	536	783	10.9
Abdul-Jabbar, L.A.	82	190	696	886	10.8
Washington, Port.	80	325	517	842	10.5
Bird, Bos.	82	216	636	852	10.4

Swen Nater

3 PT. GOALS

Minimum: 25 Made

	FG	FGA	PCT.
Brown, Sea.	39	88	.443
Ford, Bos.	70	164	.427
Bird, Bos.	58	143	.406
Roche, Den.	49	129	.380
Taylor, S.D.	90	239	.377
Winters, Mil.	38	102	.373
Grevey, Wash.	34	92	.370
Hassett, Ind.	69	198	.348
Barry, Hou.	73	221	.330
Williams, S.D.	42	128	.328

Fred Brown

OPENING GAME ROSTERS

Atlantic Division

Celtics: Parish, Archibald, *Kreklow*, M.L. Carr, Maxwell, *McHale*, Bird, C. Ford, Henderson, Fernsten, Robey.

76ers: C. Richardson, Erving, Hollins, Cheeks, C. Jones, Collins, *Toney* (injured), B. Jones, *Cureton*, M. Davis, Mix, Dawkins.

Bullets: K. Porter, Dandridge, Hayes, *Terry*, *Matthews*, Williamson, Kupchak, Grevey, Unseld, Ballard, *Mahorn*.

Knicks: R. Williams, M. Richardson, C. Russell, Cartwright, *Scales*, S. Williams, Glenn, *R. Carter*, Webster, Demic, Knight (injured), *Woodson*, Copeland (injured).

Nets: F. Walker, *L. Moore*, *D. Cook*, Newlin, E. Jordan, van Breda Kolff, Armstrong (injured), *O'Koren*, *E. Jones* (injured), *Gminski*, C. Robinson, Elliott.

Central Division

Hawks: E. Johnson, Hawes, *Shelton*, Criss, Burleson (injured), J. Drew, Hill, Rollins (injured), Roundfield, McElroy, Pellom, *D. Collins*, McMillen.

Bulls: *Lester* (injured), D. Jones, May, Mack, Theus, Dietrick, *Worthen*, *J. Wilkes*, Wilkerson, Greenwood, Kenon, Gilmore.

Cavaliers: E. Smith (injured), Randy Smith, Robert Smith, Phegley, *Kinch*, Lambert (injured), Robisch, Mitchell, Carr, D. Ford, *W. Jordan*, *Laimbeer*, Robinzine.

Pistons: McAdoo (injured), *L. Drew*, Long, Lee, Kelser, Herron, Hubbard, Tyler, Robinson, *Fuller*, Mokeski, Benson.

Pacers: *K. Natt*, Bradley, *Sichting*, J. Davis, G. Johnson, Knight, McGinnis, Edwards, Bantom, C. Johnson, Orr.

Bucks: Bridgeman, Moncreif, Evans (injured), Cummings, Marques Johnson, Lanier, Buckner, Winters, Elmore, Catchings, Mickey Johnson, Lloyd.

Midwest Division

Mavericks: Boynes, Hassett, Jeelani, Huston, LaGarde, Washington, *Allums*, Spanarkel, A. Carr, Duerod, Byrnes, *Drollinger*, Whitehead.

Nuggets: Higgs, English, *Nicks*, Roche, Gondrezick, Dunn, D. Thompson, Hordges, Hughes, *Ray* (injured), Issel, *Oldham*.

Rockets: *Garrett*, L. Johnson, Paultz, Henderson, Dunleavy, M. Jones, Murphy, Malone, Leavell, *Stroud* (injured), Tomjanovich, Reid.

Kings: P. Ford, Bennett (injured), Birdsong, J. White, Douglas, Wedman, Grunfeld, Gerard, *Whitney*, Lacey, Meriweather, R. King.

Spurs: J. Moore, Gale, J. Silas, Griffin, Restani, *R. Johnson*, *Wiley* (injured), Shumate, Corzine, Gervin, G. Johnson, Olberding.

Jazz: Dantley, Judkins, Hardy, *Duren*, Boone, McKinney, *Griffith*, Cooper, Bristow, Poquette, *Vroman*.

Pacific Division

Warriors: *Carroll*, J. Lucas, Abernethy (injured), *L. Smith*, R. White, *Romar*, L. Free, Parker, B. King, Reid, *R. Brown*, Ray, Short.

Lakers: Chones, Nixon, Holland, M. Cooper, *T. Jackson* (injured), *B. Carter*, Hardy, E. Johnson, Abdul-Jabbar, *Patrick* (injured), J. Wilkes, Landsberger

Suns: *Macy*, W. Davis, Buse (injured), A. Scott, L. Robinson, High, D. Johnson, Adams, *Niles*, J. Cook, Kramer, Kelley.

Trail Blazers: Paxon, Brewer, Bates, Twardzik (injured), Steele (injured), Hamilton, Owens, Gross, *Harper*, C. Natt, K. Washington, M. Thompson, Kunnert.

Clippers: *Brooks*, P. Smith, Taylor, F. Williams, Wicks, Pietkiewicz, Bryant, Odom, *Rank*, Nater, Walton (injured), *Price*.

SuperSonics: Shelton, V. Johnson, Bailey, Awtrey, *Hanzlik*, J. Johnson, F. Brown, *Donaldson*, W. Walker, Sikma, Westphal.

Note: Rookies in *italics*.